Rare Feathers

Also from Gunpowder Press:
The Tarnation of Faust: Poems by David Case
Mouth & Fruit: Poems by Chryss Yost
Shaping Water: Poems by Barry Spacks
Original Face: Poems by Jim Peterson

Shoreline Voices Projects:
Buzz: Poets Respond to SWARM
Rare Feathers: Poems on Birds & Art

Rare Feathers

Poems on Birds & Art

Edited by
Nancy Gifford, Chryss Yost
& George Yatchisin

Gunpowder Press • Santa Barbara
2015

© 2015 Nancy Gifford, Chryss Yost & George Yatchisin

Published by Gunpowder Press
David Starkey, Editor
PO Box 60035
Santa Barbara, CA 93160-0035

ISBN-13: 978-0-9916651-6-7

www.gunpowderpress.com

To Ganna Walska
and her legacy

Contents

Susan Chiavelli "Equinox"	11
Fran Davis "Vanished"	12
Perie Longo "The Vanishment"	13
Lucille Janssen "Bird Feeder"	14
Michelle Detorie "Flock"	15
Mary Brown "Legend"	16
Carol DeCanio "A Red Bird, Finding Itself in a Human Mouth, Reflects"	18
Gudrun Bortman "I Will Think Fire"	19
Domenica Bianca "Absence"	20
John Ridland "Cactus Sunday"	21
Sojourner Kincaid Rolle "Grand Jeté"	22
Richard Jarrette "Beatitude Conjuring Bowl"	24
John Elliott "The Font"	25
Ronald Aden Alexander "Film Noir"	26
Wendy Wilder Larsen "Unchambered"	28
John Elliott "Weave"	30
Michelle Detorie "Patterns"	32
Chryss Yost "Nest"	33
Ronald Aden Alexander "Big Nest"	34
Perie Longo "Plume Cathedra"	35
Glenna Luschei "Riddle"	36
Garth Craven "A Question"	37
George Yatchisin "Why the Mockingbird Sings"	38
Friday Gretchen "Skies & Branches Are Burdened by Blackness"	39
Melinda Palacio "Don't Stare Too Deeply into Damask"	40
Gabriella Klein "Euphorbia"	41
Susan Chiavelli "Eulogy"	42
Lois Klein "Dressed to Kill"	43
Kathee Miller "Bobe's Legend"	44
Laure-Anne Bosselaar "Extinct"	46
Gudrun Bortman "Nothing but the Echo of Their Names"	47
Christine Penko "The Loneliness of Kings"	48

Tessa Flanagan "A Flock of Haiku"	50
Jacqueline Craven "Flock"	51
Kathee Miller "Flutter and Strum"	52
Friday Gretchen "Just Another Caged Bird"	54
Lucille Janssen "Collective Past"	56
Enid Osborn "The Blue Hour"	57
Kurt Brown "Bluebirds"	58
RBS "Birdsong"	60
Emma Trelles "What Happens Next"	63
Richard Jarrette "*from* The Beatitudes of Ekaterina"	64
Fran Davis "Unfortunate Find"	65
Glenna Luschei "I Want to Come Back"	66
Chryss Yost "Shell"	67
George Singer "Font"	68
George Yatchisin "Stones Turn to Birds"	70
Fernando Salinas "Duck Hunt"	72
Kimbrough Ernest "Crows, a New Rhyme"	73
Diane August "Bravado"	74
Linda Saccoccio "Crow Medicine"	75
Enid Osborn "The Snake God Speaks"	78
Melinda Palacio "Respite"	80
Mark Whitehurst "Communion"	82
George Singer "When They Are Gone"	83
Editors' Note	87

GANNA WALSKA LOTUSLAND, a botanical nirvana in Santa Barbara, California, has been managed organically for nearly 20 years, making it a sanctuary for over 85 species of wild birds. Besides being the garden's allies in pollination and pest control, these wild birds bring music, color, charm and spectacle to the garden. Lotusland's wild birds served as the muse for the contemporary art exhibit, *FLOCK: Birds on the Brink*, curated by Nancy Gifford.

Over the millennia, and across all cultures, birds have given humans inspiration, imagery and companionship. Given their ubiquity, activity, diurnal habits, color and song, it is hardly surprising that birds feature so strongly in painting, poetry and music. Some of our most enduring cultural icons are birds, such as our national emblem, team mascots and spiritual iconography, to reflect qualities that human beings admire in birds and aspire to in themselves.

Birds have made immense contributions to human development. Domesticated and wild birds, and their eggs, have provided an important source of human food for over 10,000 years. The ecological services that they provide us, such as insect pest control, plant pollination, seed dispersal and carrion disposal, are crucial and irreplaceable.

Birds inhabit every ecosystem on Earth, at an estimate of 10,000 species worldwide. Bird species are unique in their ecology and distribution, making them susceptible to changes in their habitat. Scientists around the world monitor wild bird populations to assess the degradation of global environmental and ecosystem health.

In the past 5,000 years, over 500 species of birds have gone extinct from human causes including loss or degradation of habitat, pollution and toxic pesticides, hunting for food or feathers, wild collecting for the exotic pet trade, invasive species and climate change. At the current rate of extinction the world could lose another 1,200 species during the 21st century.

Birds inform us about the rest of the natural world and the significant implications for human welfare. By adopting sustainable practices, policies, and lifestyles, humans can bring birds—and all other species, including themselves—back from the brink.

Gwen L. Stauffer, Executive Director
Ganna Walska Lotusland

Equinox

Confused, a woodpecker descends
upon my chimney, drills
the metal flue, which yields

nothing but percussion, persistent
wake-up call in this earliest
of dawns.

Nameless birds I call little browns,
common wrens or sparrows
feather my windows,

fling themselves at the mystery
of a hardened world,
mistake their reflections

for competition, as we often do—
blaming the blameless
weather on someone or anything,

witches, curses or smokestacks.
All this, while our world tilts once
again toward the new, toward the vernal,

when we are neither leaning away
from nor toward the sun
as it hangs above the equator, lights

my windows and reveals spring's omen:
On the ledge—an egg stands on end—
small, unexplained miracle.

Vanished

Flocked
on skeleton limbs
empty bird houses
grasp their mother
tree, waiting

for the flown chance
of sky, feathered
shafts, kiss of air

doors like hollows
silence
in the nested rooms

The Vanishment

*"You can endure almost anything
as long as you can sing about it."*
—James Wright

Miracles of sky, song makers, conquerors of air,
who are we but imitators of birds. First, early speech
with clicks and whistles, a Cherokee once spoke. Later,
fastened to sails and metal wings, we rode thermals
across the seas. Pierced gravity.

Too often we lose the kindness of what holds.
Fire, drought, flood. Whole flocks
gunned down, flight paths invaded. Spilled oil.
No feathers for our caps.
Sputter and drum.

Lost and gone: softer words
than dead. We scan the heavens thinking sky
 reflects our loves. Early light, check the tremble
of leaves, surely those passed on return in halo—
hello, hello

framed here in full beauty, limb-perched, names
washed white against a quilt of color holding them. for us.
No wonder our rib cages heave in the helter-skelter of time,
air throbbing with the mourning dove's coo,
before humming one more *goodbye*—

Bird Feeder

She rises each morning to avian antics,
chattering, chuffing, somersaulting
to reach plump seeds.

Little puffed chests sing arias,
conducted by mute hands;
her language is lost and wingless.

Seizures pounce, unexpected,
cat-like, suffocating, stealing words
and dignity, a wounded bird,

My sister sits by the window
as sparrows feast on sunflower seeds,
their feathered joy gives solitary peace.

But, today is different.

The feeder is empty, the birds have left;
she follows them, uncaged,
to pierce the blue fabric of the sky.

Flock

ceiling of cages unbottomed
and rewired (rewilded)
to be adrift
in the stupid wilderness
of death, which is the failure
of our own imagination

the rescripted roof rat
re-articulated through
the logic of the owls'
guts: that's wisdom.

Legend

The Opening

How long can a man open his mouth—
a nest, the feathered flocking

in and out, counting on him to hold,

hold the egg, tongue-warmed, until
the hatch?   Careful teeth.

Keeper of twigs, regurgitated worms, the man
shuts his eyes, fights his need to make sense,

but he is not smarter than wings—
breeding takes time—stubble sprouts on his cheeks.

Mouth, do not close, do not close, do not
                              [close]

The Ache

Two in the bush, but mouth around one,
the pale man supine and eyes behind
closed lids—all jitter.

        So much work to lay
an egg, hold the mouth open as nest
the way young beaks stretch
to the worm.

        Starving mouth within mouth
—O, exaltation of larks the ache of open—
He—human & bird, landscape &

man—learns how it feels to be nested then fled.

A Red Bird, Finding Itself in a Human Mouth, Reflects

Hello red bird
of many cautions,

think it over

yes, nested
in repose between

the stalactites and mites
above, below

a ledge of tongue
now asleep

but still, you
just want to know

so you stretch
your head

higher
over the rim

then wait, then decide
to go back in

to the mouth
you now call home

I Will Think Fire

   the creator said and trusted sun's heat to crow
to bring warmth back to earth and its creatures.

Was it her then that night, blaze in her feathers,
wings splayed like black flames?

Did she fling glowing coals and darkness flared,
ribbons of fire under the moon's red eye—

kindle the trees to spit roosting birds
into the air like embers

        swirling into the timber of my home?

Absence

Who will hear this blackened absence
of flight-song?
bare remembrance—a portico of lost return
hung high with empty cage-graves,
bloodless markers under eaves
where birds might once have nested,
left instead with vestiges of their faltering
notes, dying wingbeats. Extinction.

Beyond this corridor of
death sprung-open
cage doors
dangling,

the lone call of a distant mockingbird:
its solitary echo, repository of an invisible
blight—memoria of vacant silence—
that beckons to be heard.

Cactus Sunday

This is Cactus Sunday
well I can tell you where
you can find you
a prickly pear

inside my head
that is to say my mind
with the spikes projecting
out behind

with yellow flowers
and terete joints
studded with tubercules
bearing points

also its pulpy
pear-shaped fruit
flyaway birdperch
root of my root

Grand Jeté

Go inside a stone
that would be my way
                              —Charles Simic

This flick of begin
This spark of sentience
This semblance of mingle

This worry of water
This carry of sound
This hope of profound

This murmur of prayer
This synapse of contain
This dance of air

This breath of death
not one melodious note
escapes its tomb

This wish of memory
This ponder of mourning
This bellow of hallucination

As one we begin   as many
we are strong   as one
we are stronger

This essence of remain
This breath of retain
This life of begin
This synchrony of being
This holy bind of soul
This hallowed twine of love

A flock of many
A wing of one
We soar

Beatitude Conjuring Bowl

A whirlwind wrapped in poplar leaves rose up from my street,
 slim-waisted,
deliberate as Ekaterina dancing en pointe, and revealed:

Blessed whose silence overspills, you are the conjuring bowl.

I walked into the whirling open-armed, steadied by raven and mourning dove, skinned of my battle gear, blind as a moonless blood river—

your small hands, Katja, telling me that I was secure, and the glorious trumpet of the ascended Elijah praising, and there were horses.

The Font

> *– our childhood,*
>   *a fable for fountains.*
>   Jorge Guillén

Where trees can not travel,
birds fly, their bodies bearing
the seed of a new tree.

Where we can not travel,
birds sing, their throats holding
the seed of our renewal.

Film Noir

Duckling walks into a bar,
jukebox playing "Stand
by Me." Mud-hen floozy

slow-dancing solo, webbed
feet stick ever so slightly
to a marble floor.

slap   slap, slap
slap   slap, slap

Duckling asks the barkeep,
What's on tap?
Barkeep asks for ID.

Duckling left it in his other pants.
"Out!" says barkeep.
No duck he knew ever

had money on him.
"And don't tell me to put it
on your bill. Heard

that a thousand times,"
escorts duckling out
the swinging door.

duckling peers back in.
floozy still dancing,
stage center, glances

out at him, smiles. He feels
her warm breath ruffle his neck,
stimulate his pin feathers.

slap   slap, slap
slap   slap, slap

Unchambered

She stares at the rows of crystal
lined up behind glass, the stacked plates,
the chambered nautilus inside of which
she placed a fairy with green and ruby wings.

No one else there,
she stares
at the white paper,
her pen.

From the alley four-stories below,
a constant, solitary bird song stops
then starts again. *Tshsweet   tshsweet
tschsweet   tschsweet*. She cannot translate
its timbre, warble and trill.

She cannot find the bird, not even
with her new binoculars, doesn't know
its colors, patterns and size, but no matter,

she names it "Keats,"
"begin," "first mark,"
"Beethoven," "my sweet feathered heart."
The bird's song rises

its notes amplified by the bricks'
acoustics. Tiny lungs pour out their song,
again and again and again
over the dog barks, over the traffic,
over the East River. Unanswered

notes that climb skyward, over the canopy of trees,
right through the double-paned window
to her kitchen ... *tshsweet tshsweet*

The chambered boat rocks
across a blue-lunged sea.

Raised wings make sails
to travel the breath of this unknown.

Foam salt soaks her cheeks.
Wind tangles her hair. When it stops,

dolphins push the boat toward land.
She knows them as friends as she knows

each sealed chamber
in this spiral shell
she travels on.

In the last chamber, she's stored
a red velvet, waterproofed,
purse. In it a note
written in pale-blue ink
begins: *Dear dear Bird,*

Just in case somebody ever
finds it.
Just in case, some one
is looking. *Thank you.*

Weave

Who's to say the real tree is not the roots holding
an orchard of soil in a goblet of wood, its branches
and leaves submersed in air to gather light and carbon?
We are upside down in their world, tapping their chins
from beneath with incessant footsteps, chanting our
upside-down thoughts ...

Yet branches swirl, leaves coalesce in murmuration
like starlings rising from a field. Do the leaves imitate
a convection of birds or do birds imitate leaves wrestling
with the wind? Brief leaves on a branch, birds connect
with the petioled blades in the way of all things, form
meeting form through a tenuous, emergent dance.

Beneath *Dracaena draco*, on the ground and the low
branched limbs, grey eyes, subtle and cunning, whorls
of abundant orange-tipped lashes, gather what they see
to a hidden chamber. Or are they mouths where birds
will fledge? Weeping birds left behind, seek these nests
under Dragon Trees seized from the Canary Islands.

What hunger for the nest! To find form, to weave sticks,
leaves, bark into a home against wind, storm, predators,
to soften the cup with string and down. Not mere instinct,
birds learn from disaster, rebuild a nest to hide from the
ransacking eye of a cowbird, reinforce the broken brood cup
with pliable twigs, secure the open womb on a stouter branch.

DNA is only mentor, its double-helix weaving the nest
and the weave of two species learning too slow from too
quick disasters. How can the Huia be rebuilt from the feathers
of a now unfashionable hat, or the Passenger Pigeon,
once in flocks three-hundred miles long, billions strong,
fledge and take flight from a painting by Audubon?

The hungry image, soul of bird and artist, gratification
of many, our passive eyes can't change unless we move
to a new position, to a new eye, to a way of seeing not
seen before. Bring us grace which says we are a part,
not the whole, a nest, not a destroyer. Weave us until
we are no longer predator, but tree.

Patterns

A weft of swollen shelter
glazed with imaginary rain from mercurial clouds
of resinous sourlight. The sickening pink suck
of my heart in the dark. You are always so far
away. Boy on the shore with your burnt hands
in your pockets. The wind makes a blur
in the shape of your grief. A blind
of orchard whips cured with the sad heat
of hours crawling on hands and knees
toward some bent horizon: a star slipped
against green wings shivering
where our hands made a nest of memory.
Sometimes we rest there. It's where
I turn my face
when you look away. While you're gone
I remember how we found
each other in that dome of the swallows' swoop-dart-swoop
against the gold hills of impossibility. Each day new
threads snag and snarl in the hurt branches.
I spool the switch with my own hair.
I am made of many days.

Nest

I shaped a stack of sticks into a bowl—
sticks I should have carried with my beak
or scaled four-toed feet. It was the best I could build.
My fingers are all flutter and no feather,
my legs truncheons, useless for perching.

Yet, who is blessed above the nest-maker?
To welcome every future—stork or carrion bird,
sparrow or eagle. Cupping the pregnant eggs
whatever secret song or shriek they're hiding.
This is love: awkward circular wanting,
the crack that calves a little capsule home.

Big Nest

Vanessa watches birds. She loves their beady eyes,
like onyx, those impossible feathers, their scrawny legs,
so much like her own. By her pool, near the lotus blossoms,
she built a nest lined with fern fronds, large enough
to curl up in, which she does every day before
and after her job as a screenwriter. She took eggs
from the refrigerator and stayed with them for days
over a holiday until they began to smell. She never
felt so needed. When she was fired for distractibility,
she found a job working from home, making calls soliciting
health club memberships, sat in her nest all day
with her computer and her cellphone. She bought a quartet
of footballs but they failed to give her the satisfaction
the eggs provided, so she purchased live eggs at an ostrich farm,
found out the temperature necessary to hatch them, purchased
an electric blanket for her nursery. She has taken a medical leave
from work, told her employer she has leprosy, only weeks to live.
She sits with her eggs now, night and day, waiting for them
to hatch. She cannot wait to teach her fledglings to fly.

Plume Cathedra

    A sort of a throne   to rest your bones
     if you be a Queen ruling the roost
    alas! only mere poet back out of whack
    you're invited to rest in this mimical nest
      relieve weight   off your feet
      do as your told   (no fun getting old)
    to move the plumes above your head
       breathe in   breathe out though
        feeling like lead

the harder the better   is the trick
    another try   wings snap and click
  you're off on the fly   feathered and mindful
surrounded with song   cracked open from shell
      what could go wrong

  another faint click   an idea hatching
    beyond you hear twitters and laughing
      open an eye   to your surprise
   your picture taken fantasy forsaken

     you land with a thud
    not lotus up from mind's mud
    nor large wing-flapping bird

the design of the seat   it turns out
  is to resurrect you   back on your feet
  restored rebalanced you swift

Riddle

What is the purpose of a fence?
To keep the peacock safe
from lions lurking in the grass.

To protect her from the kangaroo
loose
in the outback.

But what of a peacock tamed?
If she is maimed
can she endeavor to show her true colors?

What is the purpose of the nest?
To give the flying flock a rest
when they alight to drink.

Purpose of the empty cage?
To mourn the songbirds now extinct.
To answer the riddle: sadness, rage.

A Question

He's back.
Puffing out his rust brown chest
with a bob and dip of his jet black cap,
cocky in his smallness.
Though I always forget his name
it does me good to see him
once more take his place
in the turning of the year.

He's back too.
To sing us how it's that time again
and the Earth's alive with birth and continuity.
He sings a song that goes on and on.
till it strums the very chords of Spring

And yet
I haven't thought of them all winter.
Haven't wondered where they've gone
or if they will return.
Which leads me to the question.

If this was their last Spring,
as happened to so many more before them,
would I notice that the year had turned without them?
Would I notice that my soul had been diminished?
Lost the pleasure and awareness that they bring?
Or would I just pass on in wintry forgetting?

I look at them and listen,
hoping that I'll never
find the answer to the question.

Why the Mockingbird Sings

Perhaps I hate
the mockingbird
not for its endless
mid-night trills
its aping of alarms
its chittery
insistence but
because it mocks me.

What else do we
both have but
to sing the songs
we've heard others
more expertly
express at times
more suitable
for something like psalm?

Yet we both
sing on as if
ears want our
nonsense, or
worse, the echoes
of something
beautiful but now
merely mirrors,
the real in flight.

Skies & Branches Are Burdened by Blackness

Quiet air succumbs to squeals
and poor attempts to caw,
a low squatting body, pink gaping mouth
and furiously flapping wings
reveal another ravenous youngster

It's a new beginning—
Just weeks ago
we had dialog marked by caws and clicks
Played counting games
to acknowledge the other's existence

Now, these babies need your attention
Teach them to scavenge for themselves,
keep a keen eye for predators and
fear humans

We no longer speak, though I continue to try
These one-sided conversations make me
the crazy bird-lady of my block

I maintain clean water
chop walnuts for your murder

All the while clicking, waiting for a response

Don't Stare Too Deeply into Damask

After the oyster soup, before the aperitif,
and during a meal of stuffed quail with nuts and berries, all is quiet,
except for the tinkling of silver on porcelain and faraway voices,
human and bird, in the distance.

Human ghosts holler for love they have lost;
birds of prey screech in praise of a slow shrew.
As if quantum, damask wallpaper tears through time.
Woven patterns come alive and owls appear.
One owl winks its heart-shaped face. Eyes like pools of yesterday.

Wings flush through script and scrolls, sail through broken chair legs.
Gold and sorrow surround long halls.
The thirteenth guest, the one you did not invite, has a birdlike gaze,
quiet, but smiles too much. Bird bravado.

Dessert arrives in flames. Cherries Jubilee. A better choice
over singing magpies, baked in a pie.
A barn owl swoops down to snatch your half-eaten dinner,
swallows sweet fire instead.

Euphorbia

I want you to   eat well

I should open   your   cage

        my   mouth of feathers and

    bless

    like a childhood

               she writes

who am I becoming?   what will happen next?

      a full Beltane moon

    I should release you

               tree climber

you will have   wings

               the suffering   euphoric

      we arranged for

              rare feathers

             for your hats.

Eulogy

Madame selects the hat plumed
in extinction black. Multiplied in silvered mirrors,
she pauses to appraise a grief-trapped gaze.

Surrounded by herself in the wavering
reflections of the windows, caught
in the infinite of the lonely, mirrored hall,

her face appears Daphne-like, a vessel filled
with leafy light—crowned forever
with the memory of flight as mourning doves keen.

In her dressing room, a wayward bee. There,
again, buzzing near her feathered head, deceived.
Eyes close as she anticipates the sting.

Dressed to Kill

When feathered hats were all the rage
every woman craved one—egret,
partridge, parrot, finch perched upon
a thousand prideful heads.

From countless raided rookeries
the skillful hands of milliners left
entire litters of hollow bones,
fossils of a million murdered birds.

Mornings on the hillside by
our house a huddle of perky quail
sprint across the grass, topknot
feathers bobbling as they go—tufts of
banded amber on bouncing quills.

Afternoons, one takes to posing on
our backyard fence, his steady eye on me,
his fluttering chapeau a salute to life,
his *own*, designed and promenaded by nature,
the only milliner now allowed to claim it.

Bobe's Legend

How do I begin to find a flock of birds
in my mouth in a nest of safekeeping,
to be released as the voice freedom.

Hand on pen: how do I begin to inscribe wing
or caw onto a page, hieroglyphic of flight,
divine light, messages of wind and hunger.

Remember the lost ones, the fallen,
let wings form an alphabet of hope,
let twilight and feathers have their say,
rise out of my mouth like Janis Joplin singing
Summertime, free as a bird before all her dying.

The edges of time fold inward.
Begin again—open mouthed.
Who am I becoming? Who is leaving and for where?

How to stretch out across the rain-hungry
land that waits like an open hand,
release all I carried till now, let dust cover me.

Two ravens fly in-between the crevice of giant rocks
barking against a bleeding sky, Canterbury bells
bloom their blue tears.
From desert to shoreline I wander.

How do I begin to find my own quietude
forming like a flock of birds into a pattern

their instincts guide them into
  arrow
        cloud
                dark flower.
In limitless sky.

I blossom in silence,
dream of bird wings draped in tar and oil,
heavy-struggling to open without flight
along polluted beaches, a cathedral of horror.

How do I begin to tell you anything true?

Like that burnt sienna rock I brought home,
one black feather, a white bone, laid at the altar
on my front porch, humble prayer of surrender.

I will remember—my mouth says.
Open and close.
Open and close.

Red wings, white, black, yellow, blue.
Each song and flutter an alphabet of freedom.
Each body saved, washed and clean again
as morning.

Mourning is a river, an open cage door,
your voice, a single
truth—arising.

Extinct

Head thrown back   the man who loves birds
slowly   opens his lips & through them

slowly
                a wren
                    takes wing
& flies & flies
                        away.

I don't know if anyone heard his cry that day
or knew where his   tiny wren
                flew & flew
                            &   flew

or if she ever   sang   again —

                (did she call
                & call
                until she could   no longer?)

His wren.   Lost & last.   For she was

the last,

& no one will see her again:
        or hear the lost song
                of the San Benedicto Rock Wren.

Nothing but the Echo of Their Names

Did the lisping notes of the Bachman's Warbler
quiet an Anasazi child's cry   the reedy trill
of the San Benedicto Rock Wren
soothe an old woman's longing?

Where are they now?

Tasman Starling   Bermuda Flicker
Dusky Seaside Sparrow   where
do their songs   ripple the dawn?

Do they flit   back in time   swoop
over shivery prairies   roost
in trees left   to touch the clouds   dip
at the banks of rivers

sip untainted drops of rain?

The Loneliness of Kings

Standing in the tour group,
sunhats, bamboo parasols, cell phone cameras,
we follow our guide like a flock of geese—
but not geese—more like the duck
decoys artfully painted to meld into the river
rocks installed in the garden's hardscape.
We move on
to nests built by human hands.
No birds will inhabit these facsimiles.
Nor will we use them, only stare
and cluck with admiration.

*

We, who stand apart from all creation
viewing it—often as not—through windshields.
Yesterday, a white egret lay splayed
beneath a freeway overpass, it's long, white, neck stretched
like an arrow pointed toward the rush of tin and petroleum.

*

Gone the day of the Passenger Pigeon,
Carolina Parakeet, San Benedicto Rock Wren.
Gone the Labrador Duck, White Chested White Eye,
Imperial Woodpecker. We shall never
see again the Canary Islands Oyster Catcher
or hear the cry of the Slender Billed Curlew. Goodbye,
goodbye to the California Turkey, Buchman Warbler.
Guadalupe Storm Catcher, farewell.

*

Yet pity poor us—two-legged, big headed, sore backs, bad eyes.
Pity our sad knowledge of our brief lives.
Set apart, we suffer the loneliness of kings
even as we stand together in this tour gawking,
nodding. Tweaked with guilt, puffed with purpose,
we aim our cameras at proof of place among the rest of god's creation—

*

Will there ever be that longed for upwelling of spirits?
Like a murmuration of starlings, will we praise the day
when, freed from human bodies, we will at last be folded
into the flock from which we were so early and brutally driven?

A Flock of Haiku

Golden barn owls blaze
aloft on ivory walls,
watch us watching them.

Imprisoned behind
black bars—a bird's only chance
to survive on earth?

Crow, feathers on fire,
understands how dire the plight,
cries like peacock, "Help!"

Dismal shriek unheard,
invading rats run riot.
Laughing Owl is gone.

Door open, empty
cage. Bay Starling vanishes—
one more perfect loss.

How did this happen?
Great Auk could explain to us.
Oh, that's right. He can't.

Dragon trees weep blood,
tears that become violins.
Nest in their sighing.

Flock

Cathedral of sound in Lotusland as birds flitter and flutter
flirting in a canopy of greenly feathered light
explosion of crows spit from trees like black beryl
midst throngs of trembling trunks in a primordial underworld
hanging mosses in dappled dampness merged with nests of curly willow

Here survivors for whom the bell has not yet tolled
Inside, a requiem for birds extinct from stolen habitats
milliners, poisons, pesticides
memories of flitter, flutter and flock.
it's not too late
nurture the earth like an ailing mother
see her flourish
awaken sweet songs of the birds

Flutter and Strum

If only I could so live and so serve the world that after me there should never again be birds in cages.
—Isak Dinesen

I swore I would never cage a bird she said.
Freedom's just another word for nothing left to lose,
a song sung at Woodstock in my free flying years.

My father brought home a talking bird named Bobo,
when I was child, who spoke with a Bronx accent in a rough
and tumbled voice: *"Step to the rear of the bus!"*

On Long Island we knew cardinals, chickadees, maybe crow,
on tame blocks with tightly packed houses all in a row,
no raptors noticed then. Nothing skyward but clouds.
We had a monkey who lock-picked his way out of his enclosure.

In Manhattan years later, there were hawks that nested
among skyscrapers. I liked to dangle my feet on the ledge
of the rooftop above the 13th floor of our building,
was sure if I fell I'd fly, *Blackbird* by the Beatles played on.
Music took root, grew wings, took off.

Jimi Hendrix played his guitar in ways we
began to know from the inside out, on fire,
touched in each crevice and fold, strummed
All along the watchtower of our bodies. Rock
and roll cracked open from Elvis to Led Zeppelin,
Stairway to Heaven soared on the updraft.

There are exotic parakeets in a birdcage at Lotusland.
I swore I would never cage a bird. But here they are
fluttering on electric guitars, singing with hot desire,
Lovebirds land on metal strings, peck and strum notes
like rockstars, Grace Slick, Tina Tuner, The Who.

A lotus flower roots in mud, then rises to bloom.
Perhaps we sing louder because we are captive.
Perhaps we flutter and strum because there is already a wild
music in us just waiting. Perhaps it is always the song of
freedom we are hearing.

Just Another Caged Bird

Here,
Easter egg-colored finches fling
themselves about within six ebony fences
of iron, just missing one another
mid-air

Seed can be found everywhere
even gathered along bell bronze edges
of a drummer's cymbal, upturned

Suddenly,
a sound that would make Jimi proud—
Two electric guitars perched carefully
inside, live cables slinking to a speaker
amplify tiny bird toes plucking six-string songs
simply by landing there

But this one—
this
lone
fat
blank page-white
all chuffed-up
and nowhere
to go
bird
doesn't move a hollow bone

He's found a home on the 21st fret
too full of seed to move, and with all this
composing going on around him—
He's the perfect fluffy pillow
to muffle the collective ego
of those colorful flitting sorts

Collective Past

In dusty drawers, by dozens
laid neatly, resting, side by side
no murmuration, a silent flock

    flight interrupted

Caged, hunted, persecuted
from perch to precipice
plummeted into oblivion.

The Blue Hour

When the sun's last rays slant
and shadows are laid deep,
well before sleep, we are amazed: The crows
turn blue, float down in scores

to walk the sod with turned-in toes
and ponderous nod—very old crows
or, if not old, then droll, self-amused
crows who hold a joke between

their shoulder blades. The blue is
in the sheen. Old souls, long wings
folded, made, tips crossed, neatly austere
yet glossy, burdenless to wear.

A sangha of blue-clad, not-sad monks
in walking meditation, songless, silent,
bunkless, aimless, each crow attending
to its own line of stones. After spending

all the day maligning creatures, earth,
and sky, the crows of all birds do no harm,
but bless the ground and charm the eye.
A-shining blue the crows go 'round

in silent dharma, bowing down to sun,
to hill, to nil, to no one, to the stone.
They're here now for the blue hour;
when the blue goes, the crows go home.

Bluebirds

Forget allegory, this is a fact:
a pair of bluebirds nests each year
in the eaves of our house in Snowmass.
The male is a shocking electric blue
so you have to imagine something gaudy;
something heightened, even in nature.
Most of what we get around here
is dull, soot-soaked, dingy as old bread.
But not this fellow. He shows up
each spring with his mate.
She's muted, mostly gray, only
a thin veil of azure draped on her wings.
The two of them scope out the roof
like a pair of newlyweds, looking for a home.
For some reason the female
catches sight of our ficus tree
through the living room window.
Why not build a nest there,
in that warm palace of leaves,
and not outside in the cold limbs of an oak?
She assaults the window,
striking it again and again, flying
into her own desperate reflection.
I wouldn't call it the tree of Paradise,
but it looks pretty good to her. I wouldn't say
she was practical, or wise.
I'm only telling you this to let you know

what happens, sometimes,
in a world we often look down on.
And they're not fools. They know
what they want, gathering what they can
to fly into the face of their longing.

Birdsong

My girlfriend's father died in Europe
she couldn't be there and in spite of her usual skepticism
she asked if a Buddhist funeral could be held.
The intent is to nurture and promote rebirth in a pure land,
a psychological space free of obstacles to waking up,
or at least attaining a favorable rebirth.
Just before the last ring of the gong evanesced into silence,
a hummingbird flew in and was trapped
against the plate glass window
until one of her sons was able to snare & release it
back into the sky.

My Chi Gung teacher & Chinese doctor
said that birds are the "messengers of heaven"
if you are fortunate or rather if your spirit and mind are tamed
you can approach closer than 8 feet.
Naturally I tried to sneak up
on birds to show my wisdom and calm.

I see birds as sentinels who traverse back and forth over
invisible boundaries especially where the thin places are.
Birdwatchers report that titmice and nuthatches
are the heralds of the forest, the early warning system
for all the inhabitants.

For many years I searched ancient wisdom for answers, from sutras to
Upanishads, from apocryphal gospels to secret alphabets.
Lately I have made another turn, a 12 step program
away from texts and scriptures.

In a gap, I caught the scent of an early memory, and recalled
what one teacher proclaimed,
"Apparent phenomena are all the books one needs."

With the birds, it's not so much that they show us the difference
between how things appear to be and how they truly are.
But when they are near and you are aware,
a moment opens in the midst of stress and speed
and you glimpse the flash of feathers and color
or their soundnotes penetrate to the non-conceptual mind, as
constrictions of time and guilt and obligation disperse.
It doesn't matter if you are in a dark wood or brightest daylight
the relaxation recognizes the ubiquitous potential of no conditions.
The chirping, the effortless flight above our heads,
the defiance of gravity, pulls us out of "conflicting emotions and
primitive beliefs about reality,"
telling with a primordial animal beauty that
whatever we do
wherever we go
whoever we think we are—
those questions don't really matter.
They are just us, stumbling for a way to steer.

Then as fresh as it can be
we recollect, that beyond gods and demons, grasping and fixation
that by every breath, all is sacred.

These days, I find myself moving closer
to earth & wind, water & fire, a longing for the elements,

I try to look closely at thoughts and perceptions and heartbreak
as the fatigue with old patterns grows…
Now, I see, and hear the tittering, joyous, whistling, precious,
crowing, crying, haunting melodies of our feathered friends
who sing in harmony with seamless nature,
singing in many dialects, but a singular message with a single voice,
"Impermanence, like the imprint of a bird in the sky…
Impermanence is indestructible."

What Happens Next

For m.d.

Not as a sparrow or a saint or any
Creature of intent, in the afterlife
I'll float around as I always did
On this earth, losing one thing then another
Heart a nest tumbling eggs and hesitation
A cave of my own making.
And the choices.
Whether to ignore the red-flecked ground
Who to want, where to land, how to keep hope
Bright as a copper arrow. There's a story in here
Somewhere. Maybe it frames a city, a house, a child
Years from escape. Maybe it's more like a bridge
A way of returning to when pale hands spoke
Stay and *run* in the same arc. Deep in the dirt and mint
The foil of bees and ivory light, forgetting is what happens next
As plain as a knife, as welcome as breath.

from The Beatitudes of Ekaterina

Pulsing murmurations of starlings on the shadow-breathing air—
visual perfume, silent Benedictus, sky's corps de ballet.

Blessed are those who gather.

Guttering cries escape our plundered hearts at the Requiem.
In the grasp of the twelve-fingered fisherman passing the Peace,

hooks of faith and miracle set in my jaws—fantastic nests appear below
the Dragon Trees of Madagascar, eight foot crows among the Wine
Palms.

The Celebrant offers comfort: *Do you know there is not a word
for 'trespass' in Finland, nor in the Kingdom of Heaven?*

Katja, I remember that poor woman you were so kind to, the one
with the appalling edema who sat at her labors

in the laundromat struggling for breath—you touched the elephantine
legs, fussed with her mad hair, she laughing, you conjured

jubilating songbirds from her slack mouth. In the car you said,
A lost Stradivarius, I gave her my red lipstick.

Unfortunate Find

Hobgoblin owls my grandfather called them. Troubling birds. They returned every year to nest in his palms. Barn owls, with creamy faces almost sweet to see, like little moons. Their night shadows loped across the walls of my childhood room, bed fortified with quilts against the menace of their calls—screeches like nails raked across a chalkboard or the shock of electrified wire. They lifted from the palms to wheel on silent wings above the sleeping damask fields, talons spread to split warm flesh, turn living creatures inside out. The blood-feast swallowed hole, fur and bone vomited in pellets beneath the trees for us to find, tease out the toothpick shards and wonder at those goblin birds. They turned cannibal sometimes, bigger nestlings gobbling up the downy weaker ones, drinking sister's blood and spitting up her tender bones.

I Want to Come Back

I want to come back with a Murder
of Crows lifting our feet through fescue grass.
We gaze up at Atlas Cedar,
ice plant blue in this arboretum.

I want to come back in the Mesozoic
where murderers nest in the Cycad tree.
We survivors of the fit, pick Jurassic
fleas off the back of the Stegosaurus.

Shell

Time pries open
all it seals.

The wall of the shell yields
to the beak of the chick
jaws of the fox
edge of the cast-iron pan.

Abundance of breakfasts,
the world casts platters and nests.

The cage that captures
partners with latch that lifts
and releases.

The song in the kitchen.
The egg cracked
before the chick can sing,
before the down weaves
into feather and wing.

The insect in its egg
the egg in the nest
and the hive humming
with want and birth.

Font

When the monks sing *de profundis*
the notes step down low and lower
below the duff and leaf litter
deeper than the stubborn earthworms'
tunnels, deeper than the dens of voles
and burrowing owls and the passages
 where armadillos nurse their pups
and bee eaters brood their eggs
in the dark. When the choir chants
to praise the fundament, it lingers long
on the root note, low as the deepest
cerulean tone out of a cello's
spruce-wood mouth. Also the Om
from the lungs and lips of yogis
thrums in the gut and the marrow
emulating the voice over the waters
in the beginning when light first
quivered as particle and wave
and the luminous day raised
the grasses and the trees multiplying
into vast forests that breathed
in and out the blue air. The sky
called for wings because they suited
the air the best and beaks fitted
to the countless seeds and songs,
meant to chirr, and skraa, coo, sing
kee-oh-wee and whip-will-see.
The birds twitter and chirp

from the branches, honk, caw,
and tu-whu from the sky; chirp
pip and kree in their caves.
Together their cacophony ripples
and laces webs of sound, radiates
nets of intricate weaves looped
and cross tied like the Ojibwe
dream catchers snaring children's
nightmares, protecting them just as monks
in this eon of the fifth extinction
chant in a low reverberating drone
and then stand silent in the slower
vibrations of pulse and breath—
standing vigil for what remains.

Stones Turn to Birds

Not that nature is a stranger to camouflage,
from cuttlefish to walking sticks creatures
take on otherness without thought to hide, survive.
But this garden is not natural in the slightest
despite its growth and bloom, so these ducks deserve
a spot along a too-blue pool, beside clamshells
gaping enough to seem carnivorous, or worse, fake.
This is the wild stage-managed by an opera diva.

For it's easy not to think of what a decoy
is meant to do: look enough duck to draw
in real birds to death. Hunters mighty bored
behind their blinds – fingers like talons hooked
over triggers. And death as ever: patient, loud,
illiterate, full of philosophizing. That these are stone
lost amongst other rocks only puzzles those
of us unwilling for miracles to fly and land;
how jaded our stony hearts not to flutter in wonder
at each bird denying air its airiness. We say *hope floats*
yet hold so little of it. We are more earth than we admit,
hiding our flight for fear of being shot down.

And now I own a decoy that was my dad's, despite
his never really hunting, preferring clay birds to real.
I want to remember a story that I don't, of an artist
he liked, a trip recalled, something sentimental.
Instead after his funeral his wife left me with a box,
the decoy nested inside amidst tin tie-tacs, other stuff
I imagine sat at a drawer-bottom like pond moss,
a wealth of nothing, even empty picture frames,
a gift asking for the other way around, cheap
and almost too easy a symbol to write. But life
delights in its decoys, the dumb earth itself stone,
and we are left deciding what we can see,
what reasons we can dream for flying.

Duck Hunt

Standing beside this manmade pond
I discover several black, grey, and white
camouflaged waterfowl
sitting strategically amid the scene
Shell-shocked motionless decoys

Naturally, I search
for a mangy grey basset hound
He should be entering my periphery from the left
sniffing the warm ground
or haunched, paw over jowl, laughing.
And this is not the instinct of a hunter,
but an early Nintendo System owner

My parents had to buy me a gun
to play this game
The pistol was lightweight and
fit perfectly in my small hands
One to two pixelated 8-bit clusters
flew across our 1975 Montgomery Ward
black and white television

I had three chances to shoot
unsuspecting ducks
that seemed designed
with Lego blocks for the colorblind
Pulling the plastic trigger made
eyes gruesomely bulge,
wings convulse into painful contortions,
flickering feathers flutter—
then, lifeless Mallards fall
headfirst into a grey field.

Crows, a New Rhyme

One is for bad news
Buried in the third paragraph
Of a doctor's email.

Two is for strength.

Three is for all the little things that bothered you
Falling away.

Four is for hope.

Five is for days that almost feel normal.

Six is a thief
That swipes the rug you're standing on.

Seven lays a carpet
For the journey ahead.

Eight is for feeling anything at all.

Nine is for kindness.

Ten is rage.

But Eleven is love.

And Twelve is for wings,
The flutter of joy, today, this moment,
The only time we have.

Bravado

Silence surrounds the twelve crow silhouettes,
eight feet tall   frozen on the brink of action.

With full blue-moon's rise, they breathe into life
free from entrapments. Claws scratch with power,
beaks practice clacks and growls.

They grouse tactics while edges of their flattened bodies
round and swell under fresh feathers.

Wings ripple   they swagger—
hunger swirls-fury within them.

Night blackens.

Agitated, they murder normal crows   banquet in the dark,
chant relentless cackles—rip and smash flesh,
drink blood—eliminate the flock.

Thousands in other flocks know and will shun or kill them.

Alarmed, the shape-shifters return—flatten then freeze
before devastation feasts upon them.

Crow Medicine

peppered with Jack Spicer

Crow, Crow, Crow

Bowing on a wire
Chant for change
Bold, brash, believer
Seer of worlds seen and unseen
Wake me up from my stupor

What you don't understand are depths and shadows
They grow, my child,
though the sun covers them
in a single day

Crow, Crow, Crow

Bring on your transition magic
In iridescent blue black armor
Sure as the pupil in the eye collects light
Answers, like waves from pearl white shell
Waves deliver words via internet connection; scrutiny, scavenge, jewels, direction

The moon
Which is beautiful and shell of the earth
Streaming

Crow, Crow, Crow

Watchful, steady balance in all realms
Stardust shimmers
Mountains collapse
Intuition laden fallout blankets the earth
Midnight Kali's necklace of human skulls clangs

"What are you looking for?"
A sensible question.

Crow, Crow, Crow

Are you aware of the nuances?
Are you listening to signs?
Winter Blazes, glaciers melt
Beetles collapsing forests with flames
Tsunami meltdown radioactive Pacific glows

Marilyn Monroe being attacked by
a bottle of sleeping pills
Like a bottle of angry hornets

Crow,   Crow,   Crow

Twin towers abolished
Paranoia powdered sugar anthrax scares in NY subways
Columbine massacre, 12 students, 1 teacher, murdered
Media feeds fear of Arab terrorists
Ravaged hearts fill lust with implants

Leaves unable even to grimly seize their rightful place
in the tree of the
Heart

Crow,   Crow,   Crow

Show me the way to go home
I'm tired and I wanna go to sleep
Drop your feathers like a trail of leaves to the goddess of symbiosis
Gather your cackling choirs together
Startle this planet with your CAW, Caw, caw!

The Snake God Speaks

My beauty, I forbid your wings
to be ensnared, your feet to be tethered,
your sight to be confused by wires,
your resplendant feathers to be displayed
or worn as ornament.

I forbid you to take food from any hand but mine,
any tree but mine.

Your call will echo through the sacred forest.
Fly, *Quetzal*, over mountain,
valley, water, flock, tree and field!
Fly over my people and my enemies
and return to me!

Some have forgotten the law of the Snake God
and the Snake God himself! My curse
falls regardless upon the unknowing
poacher who casts a covetous eye,
who pursues, traps, kills, strips my nahual
of emerald plumage, dearer than money.

Such an unfortunate will suffer my wrath
without knowing why, without remembering
the covenants of the Aztec fathers.

The old gods live. We are not forgiving gods.
The old laws repeat themselves on the wind.
My bird, my *nahual*, God of the Air,
the green trees are yours, the blue lake is yours!
The sky is yours! Fly! Carry my message
to the faithful.

Respite

Your breath opens and closes feathered fans, a gift.
Wind from white ostrich wings kisses your face.

The artist considers the science of breath and flight.
Avian breath, avian flight.
Human breath, human flight.
An effort of flight and the effortlessness of human breath.
The common denominator = breath.
Breath, flight, gravity.

The poet ponders the healing aspects of breath.
Breath, anxiety gone.
Breath, insecurity forgotten.
Breath = energy begets energy.
Birds on the brink of extinction: BREATHE.

Inhale.
Exhale.

A round white light turns on. Not death, but a found poem.

The Plume Cathedra
Also Known As
Wing Chair
Breathing Chair
Angel Chair
Flying Chair
Sensory Perception Chair
Alter mass and gravity as
bird music serenades. Across the room,
a gold finch lands twang on an amplified guitar.

Begin, again.
Breathe.

Communion

Tea ceremony silence,
nature's prayer,
with huddled peace,
it begins.

Eyes upward,
a soft tornado fluttering white,
spreading and circling the forested walls.
Ascending they whisper, remember me.

A shadow cast between,
rising and swooping,
bursting upward,
lifting in harmony,
pulling hearts beyond.
Rendering, remember me.

Somber clouds join the boisterous ballet,
high the deity's head,
lost horizons no more.
Echoing, remember me.

When They Are Gone

They fly up to the sphere of celestial fire
where the souls of the vanished birds
are fashioned into gems as befits a realm
of wondrous light because jewels are suited
to what is bright the way the green
and yellow plumage of the Carolina Parakeet
once suited exactly the canopy and patches
of sunlight in leafy forests at river's edge
and the Lesser 'akialoa's scimitar
bill fitted perfectly the deep
throated o'hia blossoms. Among the genus
Gruiformes, the Layson Rail and Tongatsu
Rail are forged into Linde Emeralds
and Lynx Emeralds, the Asencion Crake
and the Saint Helena Crake, Lux sapphires
and Lynx sapphires. Inset in the endless dome,
the disappeared from the genus Galliformes:
the New Zealand Quail and the Himalayan
Quail transformed into Rose Beryl
and Rose Spinel. Of the irretrievable
Falcinoformes, the Reunion Kestrel glimmers
as Abalone Pearl and the Guadalupe Caracara,
Cortez Pearl. Despite the miracle
of the duality of particle and wave,
not everything can be mated with light.
The splendid Mandarin Garnet does not
fully capture the white feathers
of the swan sized Rogigues Solitaires
... *which lively represents ye fine neck*

of a beauteous woman... nor the way
it walked ... *meseems with such Pulchritude,
Stateliness and Good Grace, that a wight
cannot help admiring them and loving them.**
The silence there is another thing:
though it glimmers in the brilliance
as Rutilated Topaz, no one hears the crescendo
zip-note from the Bachman's Warbler once
sung from high perches in timbered swamps
with still pools. Though mounted now
as the most iridescent Fire Agate, the Huia's
haunting song (known only on earth
from a wax cylinder of Henare Hemana,
the last Maori man who could whistle it).
Of course there are good reasons for
choosing the crystalline abstraction of jewels.
The dross is poured off in the alchemy
of transmuting bird soul to gem stone.
The brilliance of the Cornflower Blue
Saphire does not preserve the whole
story of the Reunion Shelduk—how
starving Dutch sailors found they
could lure them: *If ye seized upon a popinjay
or other such... and tortured it until it*

*cried ye great gardyloo whereupon
the shelduk would fly close as if to protect
it & therefrom were easy to seize.
Betimes ten men could feed ten score in a day*.*
The tear drop pearls spread across
paradise's dome like the Milky Way,
are the souls of Passenger Pigeons
that famously filled the continent's skies
for days in a passage hunters with guns
and farmers with plows thought would
never end under the heavens.

*Journal of Willem Bontekoe (1640)

Editors' Note

FLOCK: Birds on the Brink was a contemporary art exhibition curated by Nancy Gifford and featuring thirty-five international artists responding to the theme of global loss of wild bird populations. Artworks were displayed in the galleries and gardens of Ganna Walska Lotusland in Montecito, California.

As visitors passed the Lotus Pool on their way to the main house, they may have noticed R.T. Livingston's camouflaged *Sitting Ducks: Hiding in Plain Sight-Site*, which featured hunting decoys painted to blend into the stones surrounding them. Other garden installations included an imposing oversize *Murder of Crows* in the Blue Garden, Gary Smith's human-scale nests, a larger-than-life caged topiary peacock by Joe Shelton, and *Pod Nest* by Luis Velazquez in the Pavilion Courtyard.

Also in the Pavilion Courtyard, a sound/font sculpture by Carlos Padilla replayed recordings of birds from the Amazon while visitors wandered beneath empty cages with black gaping doors labeled for extinct birds who would never return, an homage to Rachel Carson's *Silent Spring*.

Inside the Pavilion, David Hochbaum's black bird *Murmuration* swooped across the ceiling over an altered Audubon print by Penelope Gottlieb, a *Burning Crow* by Keith Puccinelli, more crows by Robyn Geddes and embellished taxidermy from New Zealand artist Karley Feaver. There are various mechanical devices by Jane Edden, Juan Fontanive, Norman Reed, the playful *Four and Twenty* bronze sculpture by Susie Read Cronin, and even a diorama by Michael Long featuring taxidermied ducklings staged in a dive bar made of found objects.

Bobe's Legend, a video by Macedonian artist Robert Gligorov, played in a dark alcove, showing birds miraculously emerging from a human mouth and flying away unharmed.

A responsive chair by Alan Macy featured large swan-like wings that fanned the sitter in time with his or her breathing. The video "Egret Dance," choreographed by Robin Bisio, played nearby. In a central aviary, live zebra finches and canaries "played" guitar, bass, and drums as they flew and landed on the instruments.

Other FLOCK artists were Sharon Beals, Lynn Brown, James Hodgson, Laurie Hogin, Nathan Huff, Philip Koplin, Pamela Larsson-Toscher, Anne Luther, Kaoru Mansour, Cheryl Medow, Tom Mielko, Liza Myers, Maria Rendon, S. Gayle Stevens, Susan Tibbles, and Esther Traugot. A more detailed description of the exhibition and artworks can be found on the Ganna Walska Lotusland website: lotusland.org

www.ingramcontent.com/pod-product-compliance
Lightning Source LLC
Chambersburg PA
CBHW020622300426
44113CB00007B/750